Fruit

Julie Haydon

Chapter 1

Fruit

We eat fruit.

Fruit tastes good, and it is good for us.

pears

plums

apples

2

Fruit grows on plants.
Some fruit grows on trees.
Some fruit grows on vines,
and some fruit grows on other kinds of plants.

oranges

grapes

strawberries

People can grow fruit in their backyards,
but most of the fruit we eat
comes from fruit farms.

Fruit Farms

There are different kinds of fruit farms.
On many fruit farms,
the plants are planted in rows.

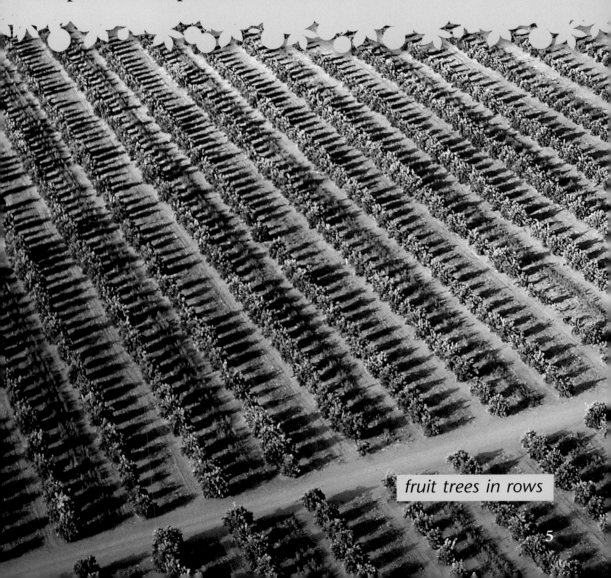

fruit trees in rows

Farmers drive big machines
between the rows of plants.
Farmers use the machines
to help them care for the plants.
Machines can be used to help farmers
pick the fruit, too.

Healthy Fruit

Chapter 3

Fruit farmers want to grow healthy fruit.
Healthy fruit grows on healthy plants.
Most fruit farmers sell their fruit.
Healthy fruit sells best
because it looks and tastes good.

healthy apples

To keep the fruit and plants healthy, farmers must:

- make sure the plants get enough sunlight
- keep the plants safe from animals and **diseases**
- give the plants water and plant food

Fruit plants need water.

- cut dead or broken branches off the plants
- get rid of weeds and grass that grow near the plants
- pick the fruit when it is ready

This farmer is picking pears.

Chapter 4

New Plants

Big, strong fruit plants grow healthy fruit.
Fruit farmers want new fruit plants
to grow big and strong quickly.

Fruit farmers can grow plants from seeds,
but this can take a long time.
Most fruit farmers plant young fruit plants.

young fruit plants

Flowers

When the fruit plants are old enough,
they grow flowers.
The flowers will turn into fruit.

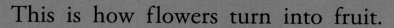

This is how flowers turn into fruit.
1. A yellow powder called pollen
   is made inside flowers.
2. Pollen sticks to insects or is blown about
   by the wind.

pollen

3. The insects and the wind carry the pollen
   from one flower to another flower
   of the same kind.

4. This makes seeds grow inside the flower.
5. Part of the flower turns into a fruit.

6. The fruit has the seeds inside it.

Chapter 6

Apples

There are different kinds of fruit.

Apples grow on trees.
They have a thin red, green, or yellow skin.
The inside of an apple is called the **flesh**.
The flesh of an apple is hard and crunchy.

There is a core inside apples.
There are small hard seeds in the core.

core

You can make a tasty snack.
Ask your mom to cut up some apples . . .

Oranges

Oranges grow on trees.

They have a thick orange skin.

The flesh is in **sections** that can be pulled apart.

The flesh of an orange is juicy.

Only some kinds of oranges have seeds inside them.

seeds

Then peel and cut up some oranges . . .

17

Plums

Plums grow on trees.
They can be many different colors.
Plums have a thin skin.
The flesh of a plum is soft.

There is a stone inside a plum.
The seed is inside the stone.

stone

Then cut up some plums.
She will have to take the stones out . . .

Grapes

Grapes grow on vines.
They can be many different colors.
Some grapes have a thin skin.
Some grapes have a thicker skin.
The flesh of a grape is **firm** and juicy.

Only some kinds of grapes have seeds inside them.

seeds

Then add some grapes . . .

21

Strawberries

Strawberries grow on strawberry plants.
Most strawberries have a thin red skin.
The flesh of a strawberry is firm.